THE ADVENTUR
ODYSSE

A Greek legend adapted by Gill Munton

Series Editor: Louis Fidge

Contents

Odysseus's journey		3
1	The Lotus Eaters	4
2	A monster in a cave	7
3	Wind in a bottle	12
4	Giants	16
5	Penelope's tapestry	19
6	A strange drink	23
7	A deadly song	28
8	Monsters of the sea	32
9	Odysseus and Calypso	37
10	Where is Odysseus?	42
11	Father and son	46
12	The last feast	50
13	A shooting contest	54
The Sea		58
Ancient Greece		60
Greece today		62

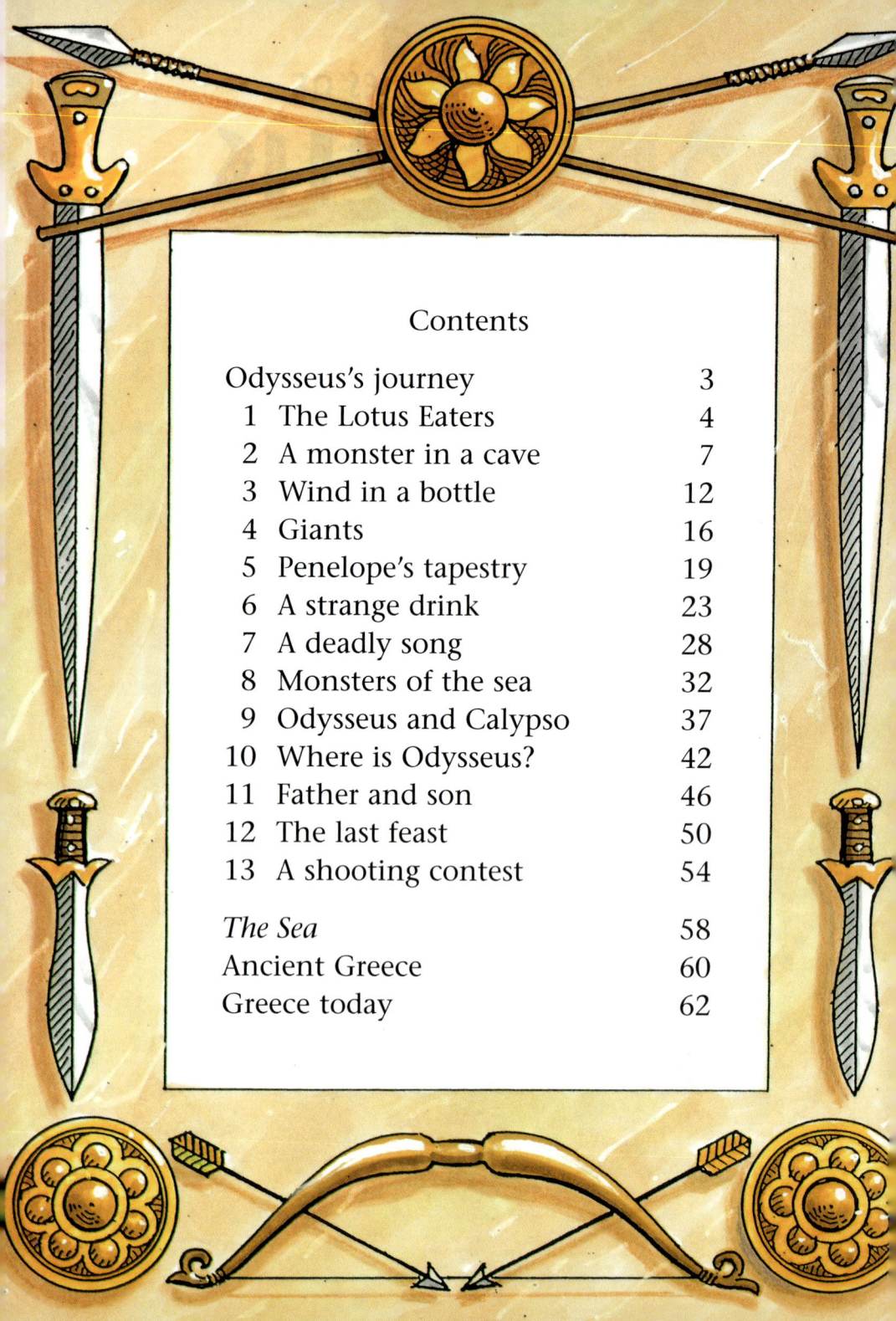

ODYSSEUS'S JOURNEY

The story of Odysseus was first told in Greece almost three thousand years ago. Greece is a country in Eastern Europe. It has more than three hundred islands.

Odysseus was King of Ithaca, one of the Greek islands. He and his men went to war with the people of Troy. They won the war, and filled their ships with treasure. But the journey home was long and difficult …

CHAPTER 1
THE LOTUS EATERS

Twelve ships sailed away from Troy. Odysseus stood on the first ship. He looked straight ahead, towards Ithaca.

'We're going home – to Ithaca!' he cried.

His men shouted and cheered.

Soon, they came to a small island.

'We must stop for some water,' called Odysseus. The men pulled the ships up the beach. 'You three! Go and see what you can find!'

The three men set off to look for water. The others took down the ships' sails and went to sleep.

Odysseus was worried when the three men did not return. He picked up his sword and went to look for them. As he walked up the beach and into the forest, he saw some little blue-and-yellow flowers.

Odysseus stopped, and looked again. Yes, he was right – they were lotus flowers! He was in the land of the Lotus Eaters!

Now Odysseus knew why the three men had not come back. The Lotus Eaters were very friendly. They gave food and water to people who came to their island. But the food was always made from lotus flowers – and lotus flowers made you forget! When you ate lotus flowers, you forgot your home, your mother, your father, your children – everything!

Soon, Odysseus saw the red-gold light of a fire. He walked through the forest towards it.

About twenty Lotus Eaters lay around a big fire. They were sleepy after eating the blue-and-yellow flowers.

The three sailors were there, too.

'Get up!' said Odysseus. 'Get up, and come back to the ships with me!'

One of the men woke up, and got to his feet.

'Who are you?' he asked Odysseus. 'And what do you want? You speak of ships – what ships? Go away, and leave us alone!'

Odysseus was angry now. With the strength of ten men, he dragged the three sleepy sailors back to the ships.

'We must leave this place,' he thought, 'before any more of my men forget who they are.'

CHAPTER 2
A MONSTER IN A CAVE

It was night when they arrived at the next island. In the morning, they saw green trees, flowers, and golden cornfields.

Odysseus's men were very hungry and thirsty.

'We will find food and water here,' said Odysseus.

Twelve men left the ships and went with Odysseus. Soon they came to a very big hole in the hillside.

'It's a cave!' said Odysseus. 'Perhaps someone lives here! Sssh!'

The twelve men and Odysseus walked into the cave. Suddenly, they heard some sheep. At the back of the cave, they saw them. There were about a hundred sheep.

The men found lots of good food, too.

'Let's take it all back to the ships!' said one of the men.

But Odysseus said, 'No. You may eat just a little of the cheese. I want to find out who lives in this place. We may make friends with him.'

As night fell, the hillside started to shake. Odysseus picked up his sword.

Crash! Crash!

A monster with huge, hairy feet walked into the cave!

At first, the monster did not see Odysseus and his men. It started a fire, and dragged a huge rock across the mouth of the cave to make a door.

Then it saw Odysseus. 'Who are you?' it yelled. 'Don't you know that this cave is my home? Why are you here? And why are you eating my food?'

The monster was huge. It had arms and legs like hairy trees. But that was not the worst thing. The worst thing was its one huge eye – right in the middle of its forehead!

Odysseus knew that this was a Cyclops!

'We are G-Greek sailors,' he said, 'on our way h-home from T-Troy. We are on this island b-because we must have f-food and w-water. Will you help us?'

'I will not!' yelled the Cyclops. 'I will not help Greek sailors – but I *will* eat them!'

The terrified men looked at the monster's big black teeth. 'Heh-heh-heh!' The monster laughed and then lay down. 'But first I must sleep,' it said, and shut its one eye.

When the Cyclops began to snore, Odysseus ran across the cave. He picked up a burning branch from the fire, and pushed it into the face of the Cyclops.

'*Aaaaaaargh!*'

The Cyclops screamed. It jumped up and ran round the cave. It crashed into things and yelled in a voice that sounded like thunder.

'I can't see! I can't see! Where are you? You must be punished!'

It felt around the cave with its huge hairy hands. 'Where are you? When I catch you, I will … I will …'

But Odysseus and the sailors were too fast for the Cyclops.

'You will not catch us!' they called out, as they ran from the monster. But they could not leave the cave because of the huge rock.

They ran round the cave until the Cyclops was exhausted. And then, when it was asleep again, Odysseus made a plan.

In the morning, Odysseus watched as the monster woke up and had something to eat. As it ate, it yelled.

'I am blind! I can't see my food. I can't see my sheep. I can't see my hand! What good is an eye if it can't see? I will never be happy again!'

One of the men started to speak, but Odysseus said, 'Sssh!'

'I must let the sheep out to find food,' said the Cyclops.

It went to the mouth of the cave and dragged the rock away. As the sheep ran out onto the hillside, the monster touched the wool on the back of each one and counted them. It heard the sound of their feet, but it did not see them.

And it did not see Odysseus and his twelve sailors. Each man hid under a sheep, clinging to its wool as it ran out of the cave.

CHAPTER 3
WIND IN A BOTTLE

Odysseus and his men ran back to their ships and set off again. Before long they came to another island, which seemed to float above the water.

Odysseus and his men pulled their ships up onto the beach, and walked towards a golden palace. A tall man, with red cheeks and golden hair like a lion, came to the door.

'I am King Aeolus!' he said. 'Come into my palace, and have some food with me!'

King Aeolus and his family made them very welcome, and they stayed in the golden palace for many days. Each night, Odysseus told the King about his adventures in Troy.

But one day, Odysseus started to think about his home in Ithaca, and his wife Penelope.

'It is time for us to leave,' he said to King Aeolus.

The King looked surprised.

'Leave?' he asked. 'Don't I look after you well?'

'You do,' said Odysseus, 'but I have not seen my home or my wife for a long time.'

'Very well,' said the King. 'But let me do one last thing for you, Odysseus. Let me put the winds into a bottle. Then they will not blow your ships off their course.'

The next morning, King Aeolus put a leather bottle into Odysseus's hand.

'Here you are!' he said. 'I have counted them. They are all in here – all except one light wind to help you on your way. Goodbye, my friend.'

That night, when Odysseus was asleep on his ship, one of his men found the leather bottle.

'What has Odysseus got in here?' he said. 'More treasures from Troy? Perhaps this bottle is filled with gold – gold that he does not want to share with us!'

'Let's open it and see!' said another man.

As soon as the bottle was open, the winds escaped and rushed out with a mighty sound. The twelve ships started to rock. One wind blew them one way, another wind blew them another way.

Odysseus woke up, and was angry with his men – but he could do nothing to stop the winds. By the time their battered ships were blown back to King Aeolus's island, they were all exhausted.

And this time, King Aeolus was *not* happy to see them.

'You are a fool, Odysseus!' he said. 'I gave you the winds in a bottle, but you did not look after it. You went to sleep! Off you go! You will get no more help from me!'

CHAPTER 4

GIANTS

For six days and six nights, Odysseus's twelve ships were battered by stormy seas. The winds from the bottle blew with all their strength, and the men had to take down the sails and use the oars.

Odysseus was angry with himself.

'Why was I such a fool? Why did I go to sleep? Now we will all die – and it's my fault!'

But on the seventh day, the water was calm.

One of the men called, 'I can see land! Look, Odysseus! We are not going to die after all!'

They found a harbour. Odysseus sent eleven of the ships into it so that some of the men could go and look round the island. Odysseus stayed on his own ship, out on the open sea. He was exhausted.

Three men set off to explore. After several hours, one of them returned to Odysseus's ship with terrible news:

'We saw a girl. She was filling a water bottle from a little stream. She seemed friendly, Odysseus! We had no reason to fear her. But there was one strange thing about the girl – she was so tall! She showed us the way to a royal palace.

'We thought the girl was tall! But the king and queen were as tall as trees! They were like giants! The king picked up my two friends, and opened his mouth …

'That's when I ran away. I ran as fast as my feet would carry me – out of that terrible place, past the stream and all the way back to the harbour. I knew that I had to tell you what happened, so I jumped into the sea and swam to your ship. There was no time to put up sails, or to …'

Suddenly they heard a terrible crashing, splashing sound. 'It's coming from the harbour!' said Odysseus.

They looked back at the eleven ships – but by now there was little left of them. On the hillside above the harbour, giants were hurling rocks, as big as houses, onto the ships below! Eleven ships, and many, many men were lost.

Odysseus told the men on his ship that they must leave, right away. As the wind filled the sails, Odysseus's ship set off once more – alone now.

Odysseus wept. He wept for his lost men, and his lost ships. He wept for his wife Penelope, who was waiting for him at home. Would he ever see her again?

CHAPTER 5
PENELOPE'S TAPESTRY

Back in Ithaca, Penelope worked on a tapestry of blue and red flowers, as she waited for news of Odysseus.

As she worked, she could hear music and the sound of laughter from the great hall below. The palace was filled with people who called themselves Odysseus's friends but did not want to work. They just wanted to eat and sing!

Penelope was thankful that she had many trustworthy servants, but some of the others had become lazy, too. She wished Odysseus was home again. He would soon send those lazy people away!

'I must be thankful that I still have my son,' she told herself.

But Telemachus was just a boy. A brave boy, but still just a boy. He couldn't make the lazy people go away, as his father would …

The door to Penelope's little room opened with a crash.
'Mother!'
Telemachus ran into the room. His dark eyes were wide with fear.
'What is it, my love?'
'Those men in the great hall! I don't like them! They push me, and laugh at me – and now two of them want to speak to you! What do they want?'
Penelope put down her needle and touched his hand.
'Let them come up,' she said. 'It will be all right.'
There was the sound of footsteps on the stairs. Two men came into the room.
'Penelope!' the first man said. 'Marry me! Our marriage will make me the happiest man in the world!'
'Don't listen to him, Penelope! *I* am the man for you! You must be *my* wife!' said the second man.
Penelope looked at them.
'But I am Odysseus's wife,' she said.
'Odysseus? The war in Troy has been over for more than five years – so where is he?' one of the men asked.
'I'm sure that Odysseus will come back,' said Penelope.
'No – he will not!' the second man replied. 'Everyone agrees that he must be dead!'

Penelope began to work on her tapestry again. She was afraid to think that Odysseus was dead – five years *was* a long time. But she could not give up hope. Quickly, she thought of a plan to make the men go away.

'Do you see this tapestry?' she said. 'While I am working on it, I will think about what you have said. And when it is finished, I will give you my answer.'

The two men laughed and went back down the stairs. They were happy to wait until the tapestry was finished.

Penelope turned to Telemachus.

'Now, go and play for a while before you go to bed.'

Telemachus did not really understand what the men and his mother had talked about. But as he played, he soon forgot about the men, and began laughing again.

Later that night, when Telemachus was asleep in bed, Penelope picked up her tapestry and her needle. By the light of a candle, she unpicked a big red flower – all the work she had done that day.

'I will sew that flower again tomorrow,' she said to herself, as she blew out her candle. 'And then I will unpick another. Those men will have to wait a very long time for my answer!'

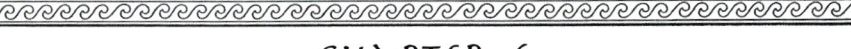

CHAPTER 6
A STRANGE DRINK

It was a long way to the next island. Odysseus and the forty-six men who were left were exhausted and cold when they staggered onto the beach. For two days and two nights, they just lay on the sand. They were too tired to move.

The next morning Odysseus picked up his spear, and went to look for food. He was lucky – he soon found a deer, which made them all a good dinner.

As they ate, Odysseus said, 'I have found one deer, so there must be more. And I think someone lives on this island, because I saw some smoke above the trees.'

The men split into two groups, and one group went to explore.

Back at the ship, the sailors in Odysseus's group waited for the others. As the sky grew dark, one man ran out of the trees and down the beach.

'Odysseus, you must do something! The other men – twenty-two of them – have been … have been …'

He stopped speaking, and wept.

'Tell me what has happened!' said Odysseus.

'We ... we found a big white house. All around it, we saw animals – lions with golden manes, and wolves! We almost ran away, but then one of the wolves came up to me and lay down at my feet!

'Then we heard a woman singing – oh, such a beautiful song! We looked through the window, and some of the men called to the woman inside. She came to the door, and gave them food and water to drink. Well, it looked like water. But it can't have been, because the men were soon half-asleep.

'Then she said some strange words – and turned them into goats! They are still there, at the white house!'

Odysseus ran up the hill with just one thought in his head: he must help his men.

As he came near to the house, a boy jumped out of the trees.

'You must be careful, Odysseus!' he said. 'That woman will turn you into a goat, too, if you don't let me help you! I will give you this white flower. Eat it, and she will not hurt you.'

Odysseus ate the flower.

A woman opened the door. She was beautiful, with long black hair.

'You look exhausted,' she said. 'Drink this – it will make you feel better.'

Odysseus took the cup, and drank.

The woman laughed, and her dark eyes flashed.

'Now I will turn you into – a goat!' she said.

Odysseus laughed.

'No, you will not!' he said as he pulled out his sword. 'Your strange drink can't hurt me!'

The woman looked at him. There was fear in her eyes.

'Take me to my men,' said Odysseus.

The woman took Odysseus to her barn.
'Here they are!' she said.
Odysseus looked at the twenty-two goats, who looked back at him with yellow eyes.
'Turn them back into men!' said Odysseus, his sword still in his hand.
The woman went into the barn and put her hand on the back of each goat. At once, the hair fell from the animals and they stood up on two feet. They were men once more!
The men wept with happiness.
'Odysseus!' they cried. 'How can we thank you?'

CHAPTER 7
A DEADLY SONG

The men laughed and sang: the ship was travelling fast, and they would soon be home.

But Odysseus did not laugh or sing. He knew something that the other men did not: they were near the island where the terrible Sirens lived.

Suddenly, the wind stopped blowing. The men took down the sail, and picked up their oars.

Odysseus told them about the song of the Sirens.

'My friends,' he said, 'we have been tested before. But this time, we will need all our strength. As we get nearer to this island, you will see the Sirens. They have the heads of women and the wings of birds! You will hear a beautiful song. You will want to go to the Sirens – but you must not! And *I* must not! I want you to tie me to the mast, so that I can't leave the ship.'

Odysseus took some beeswax, and told the men to put it in their ears so they could hear nothing. Then they tied him to the mast with a long rope.

The first thing they saw on the island was a pile of bones.

'Any sailor who sets foot on that island will soon be a dead man!' Odysseus said to himself.

The Sirens sat on the rocky shore. They were beautiful, with long red hair and blue-green wings. They started to sing:

> *'King Odysseus, hero of Troy,*
> *Come to our island, golden-haired boy!*
> *Don't let your men take you sailing past –*
> *Untie yourself from your ship's tall mast!*
> *You've been at sea for much too long!*
> *Come and hear our Sirens' song!*
> *King Odysseus, hero of Troy,*
> *Come to our island, golden-haired boy!'*

The men could not hear the song because they had beeswax in their ears. But Odysseus heard it – and he wanted to hear more. He pulled at the rope that tied him to the mast.

'Untie me, untie me, and let me go to the Sirens!' he cried. 'The more I hear their song, the more I like it!'

But of course, the men could not hear him. They rowed with all their strength – in, out! in, out! – until the ship had passed the island, and Odysseus could hear the song no more.

Only then did the men take the beeswax out of their ears. Then they untied Odysseus.

CHAPTER 8
MONSTERS OF THE SEA

'We escaped the Sirens,' said Odysseus, as the wind blew their ship along, 'but something more terrible is waiting for us. Two sea monsters! The first one has twelve legs, six necks and six heads, with three sets of teeth in each one! If a ship sails too near, he …'

As Odysseus was speaking, the ship started to rock.

'Row!' he cried. 'Row as fast as you can!'

The waves grew bigger and bigger, and it took all the men's skill to keep the ship afloat.

They saw two tall cliffs, and a dark cave.

'That is where the six-headed monster lives,' Odysseus told them. 'He may be sleeping now. But if I have to, I will fight him!'

He picked up his sword, and watched the cave carefully as his men rowed past.

'Let us give thanks!' cried one of the men. 'We are safe!'

'We have passed the first sea monster,' said Odysseus. 'But don't forget the second one. She is a whirlpool! She can pull a ship down into the water as if it were just a piece of wood!'

Then the ship started to rock, and to shake, and they heard a roaring sound. The water started to spin. The ship was being pulled into a terrible whirlpool!

'Row, men, row!' cried Odysseus. 'Or our ship will be pulled down into that awful place!'

And then they heard a terrible sound.

'It must be a giant dog!' cried one of the men.

'No dog sounds like that,' said Odysseus. 'It's coming from the cave – it must be the six-headed sea monster!'

They could not sail away from the sound – it took all the men's strength to stop the ship being pulled down into the whirlpool. The dog-like cries got louder and louder. Suddenly, six long necks reached out of the water. Six huge mouths opened wide, showing eighteen sets of sharp teeth.

Odysseus watched as man after man was snatched up by the monster, and thrown into the sea.

'Odysseus! Odysseus! Help us!' the men cried.

But it was no good. The monster was too strong. Odysseus's sword was no use, and the men could not help themselves.

Those men who were left on the ship used their last bit of strength to row the ship away from the whirlpool.

The ship travelled on. As they rowed, the men tried to forget the terrible thing that had happened. But soon the sky turned black, and a cold wind began to blow. Thunder roared and lightning flashed in the sky. Rain poured down. The men were now fighting the worst storm of their lives!

The mast snapped in two as the waves threw the ship high into the air, and turned it right over. All the men were thrown into the sea, and drowned. Odysseus managed to hold on to the mast. He was the only one to survive.

Rain and tears ran down Odysseus's cheeks. What could he do now? He clung to the wreck of his ship and tried to think.

Odysseus managed to grab some bits of wood from the wreck, and tie them together with rope to make a raft. It was small, but it was better than nothing.

All night, the storm threw the raft this way and that. Odysseus was terrified.

When it was light, he saw that he was back at the cliffs where the sea monsters lived! A small olive tree grew out of one of the cliffs. Odysseus grabbed at one of its branches and pulled himself up.

And then the sea started to rock, and spin. Odysseus looked down into the whirlpool as it pulled his little raft down, down, into the deep, dark sea.

When the waters were calm again, Odysseus let go of the branch and fell into the water. He was carried along by the waves for ten days and ten nights.

CHAPTER 9
ODYSSEUS AND CALYPSO

On the eleventh day, Odysseus was washed up on the beach of an island. He was more dead than alive.

'I have been in the sea for a long time,' he thought. 'I am so cold!'

He sat up, and started rubbing his feet to warm them.

When he looked up, he saw a girl in a long white cloak. She was looking down at him.

'She is the most beautiful girl I have ever seen!' thought Odysseus.

The girl said, 'My name is Calypso. Let me take you to my parents' home, and we will look after you.'

It was like a dream to Odysseus. The girl took him to her house on the hillside. Inside, a fire was burning, and he could smell fish cooking on a grill. Calypso's mother turned from her cooking to look at Odysseus, and her father helped him to a seat near the fire.

'Mother, Father, I found this poor man on the beach. I think he has been in a shipwreck.'

'Sit and warm yourself,' said Calypso's mother. 'And then I will give you something to eat.'

When they had eaten, Calypso's father took Odysseus to an upstairs room and gave him some clean, dry clothes.

'You can stay with us for as long as you like,' he said.

Life with Calypso's family was good. Her father caught plenty of fish, and her mother made the best bread Odysseus had ever tasted. In the afternoons, he and Calypso walked in the orchards, picking peaches and grapes.

After dinner, the four of them sat and told stories. Calypso and her parents loved to hear Odysseus talking about his adventures at sea. Sometimes Calypso sang songs for them, and it was easy to fall asleep after hearing her lovely voice.

Odysseus stayed with Calypso's family until he was strong and well again. One morning, Calypso saw him looking out to sea. He had tears in his eyes.

'You have all been very kind to me,' he said. 'But I cannot stay here any longer. I have a wife and a son in Ithaca, and I love them very much. I must go home, Calypso!'

Calypso started to cry.

'You can't leave now!' she said. 'You are my only friend, Odysseus!'

'I will never forget you,' Odysseus told her. 'But I must go.'

Calypso wept and wept.

'If you stay here, you will never become old!' she said. 'You will be a young man for ever – you will never die!'

Odysseus thought about this for a long time.

Then he said, 'If I stay, I will never see Penelope and Telemachus again! Or my home, Ithaca! If you are my friend, you cannot ask such a thing!'

'Very well,' said Calypso sadly. 'I can't make you stay. But let me help you to get ready for your journey.'

Odysseus and Calypso's father made a little wooden boat, and Calypso and her mother made a tall white sail. Then Calypso gave Odysseus a leather bottle filled with water from her stream.

'Goodbye!' she cried, as Odysseus pushed the little boat out to sea. 'May you reach Ithaca soon!'

CHAPTER 10
WHERE IS ODYSSEUS?

Back in Ithaca, Penelope's tapestry was still not finished. The men who wanted to marry her were becoming impatient.

Telemachus heard the men's conversations with his mother. He was now a young man of seventeen, and he was angry. These men said they were his father's friends – but they were not! All day long, they ate Odysseus's food and danced in his palace. And now they wanted to marry his wife!

Telemachus could not believe his father was dead. Without telling Penelope, Telemachus set off in a ship with some men to look for Odysseus. He went to visit the king and queen of Sparta, to see if they had heard anything about his father. They were his father's real friends.

When Penelope's admirers found out that Telemachus had gone to find Odysseus, they were worried.

'We must stop that boy!' cried one man. 'Let's set a trap for him! His ship will go past the rocky island of Asteris. Let's wait for him there!'

It was time for Telemachus to leave Sparta.

'Thank you for your kindness,' Telemachus said to the king and queen as his ship was loaded with presents. 'If I find my father Odysseus, I will tell him how well you have both looked after me.'

'You *will* find him,' said the king. 'I haven't seen him for many years, but I have a feeling that he is still alive. Goodbye, and good luck!'

The ship left Sparta and sailed back towards Ithaca. Telemachus thought about his mother, waiting and waiting for his father to come home.

It began to get dark.

'I can see the island of Asteris!' cried one of the men on Telemachus's ship.

'We must be very careful,' said Telemachus. 'It is a rocky island. And it will soon be night. Each of you must work hard. No one must speak until we are safely past the island.'

Wind filled the sails of the boat, and they did not need to use the oars. Under a moonless sky, the ship sailed silently past the island of Asteris and on towards Ithaca.

On another ship, behind some rocks, other men waited. They waited for Telemachus to reach the island. But their trap did not work. It was so dark, and Telemachus's ship moved so silently, that they could not see it or hear it.

When Telemachus and his men arrived back in Ithaca, they took down the sails and unloaded the ship. Telemachus was happy to be back, but he wasn't ready to go home to his father's palace. First, he wanted to find out what had happened while he was away.

'Take these presents to the palace, and give them to my mother Penelope,' he told his men. 'Tell her I am back.'

Then he walked up the rocky hillside behind the beach.

He came to a shepherd's hut. Inside, he found an old man. He was cooking soup over a fire. When the old man saw Telemachus, his eyes filled with tears.

'Telemachus! You have come home to Ithaca!' he cried.

Telemachus hugged the old man.

'I am home, safe and well!' he laughed. 'It is good to see you, my friend. Now, have you got a bowl of soup for a hungry young man?'

CHAPTER 11
FATHER AND SON

The wind started to blow, and Odysseus's little boat was thrown about on the blue-black waves. At last, he reached an island – but the cliffs were high, and there was nowhere to land. The waves smashed the boat against the cliffs, and it broke into pieces.

Odysseus swam for two days and two nights. Then he found a sandy beach, and swam ashore. He made a bed from olive leaves next to a little stream, and went to sleep.

'Who are you?'

Odysseus rubbed his eyes and sat up. A boy was looking down at him.

'I am just a sailor on his way home,' said Odysseus.

'My father is king of this island,' the boy said. 'He and my mother will help you.'

The boy took Odysseus to meet his father. The king liked Odysseus. He gave him dinner, and then he said, 'There is nothing more to fear, my friend. My sailors will take you home in my best ship.'

When the ship was ready, the queen brought some food and clothes for Odysseus. Soon, he was back at sea. He was very tired after his adventures. Before long he fell fast asleep.

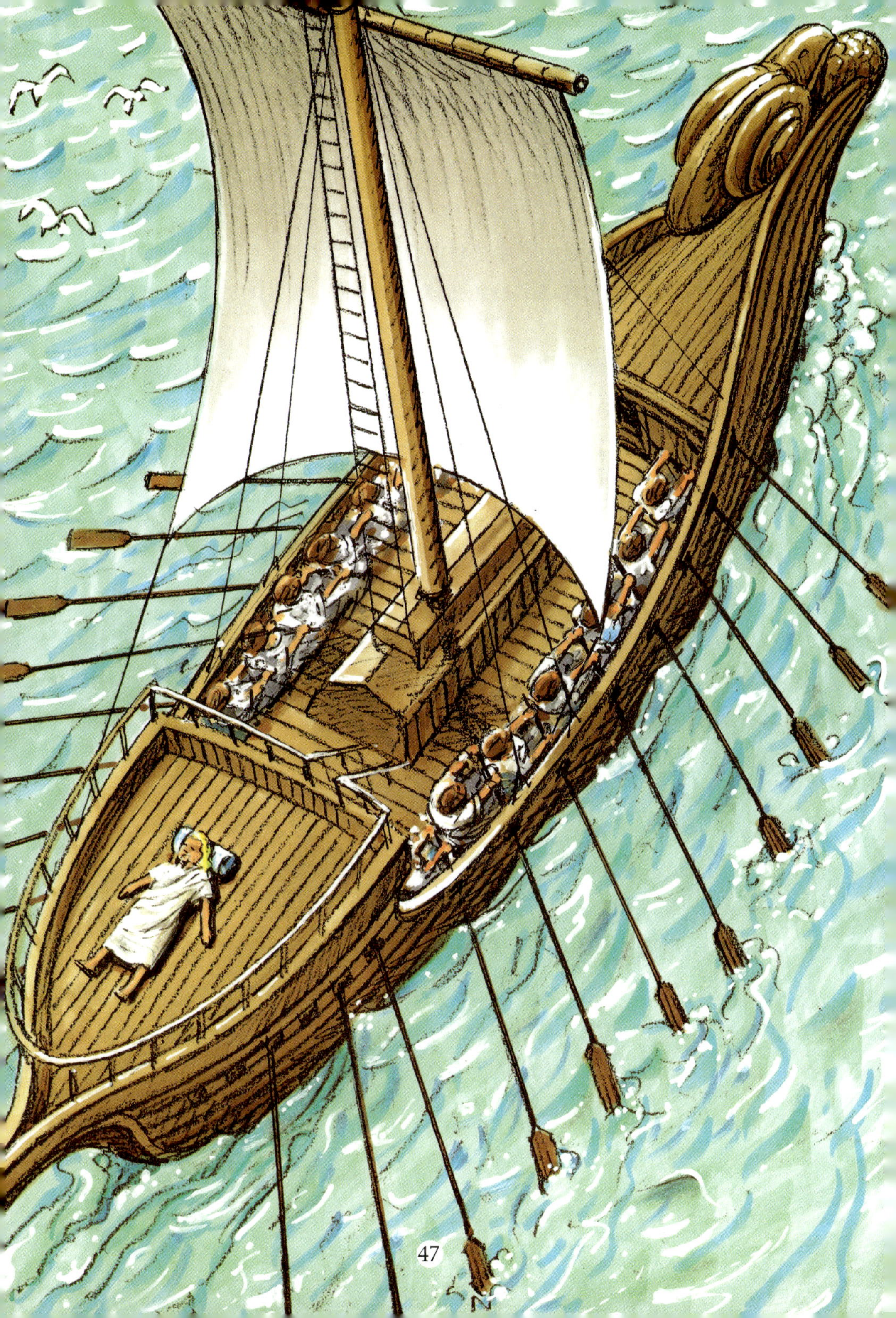

Odysseus was still asleep when the ship reached Ithaca and the sailors put him on the beach. He was so tired that he did not wake up. The sailors left him on the sand and sailed away.

'What's happening?' he thought, when he woke up. Then he remembered. 'The king's sailors must have put me here.'

He walked up the rocky hillside behind the beach. He saw a little shepherd's hut.

'Will you tell me – where am I?' Odysseus asked the old man who sat inside.

'You are in Ithaca, of course!' the shepherd replied.

Ithaca! He was home at last!

'But Ithaca has changed,' the old man went on sadly. 'Years ago, King Odysseus went away to war, and now his palace is full of lazy guests. Day and night, they sing and dance and eat the king's food. His wife, Penelope, is still hoping that Odysseus is not dead and will come home!'

A tall young man came into the hut. He was carrying a basket of wood for the fire.

'Put the wood over there, Telemachus. How strange! I have had two visitors in one day!' laughed the old man.

Odysseus stared at the young man. Was this his son Telemachus? In the time Odysseus had been away, his boy had become a man! Odysseus saw that Telemachus had big, dark eyes, just like Penelope.

The old man went off to gather his sheep. As soon as he and Telemachus were alone, Odysseus said, 'My son! I am your father, Odysseus!'

'But my father has been away for many years! Everyone except my mother believes he is dead!'

'I am alive, Telemachus. And I have come back. I have heard all about the lazy guests in the palace who take my food and want to marry my wife. Together, you and I will stop them. But we will have to be clever …'

CHAPTER 12
THE LAST FEAST

Telemachus left Odysseus with the shepherd and went back to the palace. When he got home, his mother was crying.

'You are back, Telemachus! I have been so unhappy! Those men were very angry with you when you went to look for your father. I was very worried about you!'

Telemachus hugged his mother. He told her servants to leave the room. When they had gone, he said, 'I have some good news for you – my father is alive and on his way home. But do not say a word to anybody!'

He did not tell Penelope that Odysseus was already on Ithaca. When the time was right, his father would come back to her.

That night, the lazy guests were having a feast as usual. As they ate and drank, they told jokes and listened to music. Telemachus sat with them. They were not angry with him any more, because they didn't think he had found Odysseus.

Suddenly, the music stopped and all the men stared at the door of the great hall. A beggar stood there, in the light of the moon, with a begging bowl in his hand.

'Will you give some food to an old beggar man?' he said.

Telemachus wanted to laugh. He knew that under those ragged clothes, the 'beggar' was his father, Odysseus.

'Why would we put food in the mouth of a beggar?' asked one man. 'Go home – if you have a home!'

'I have not always been a beggar,' said Odysseus. 'I was once a king!'

The men laughed.

'And another thing,' said Odysseus. 'You speak of food, but the piece of meat in your mouth is not yours, is it?'

The man grabbed a cup, and threw it at Odysseus.

'Leave him alone!' cried another. 'He's only a beggar. Let us continue with our feast!'

Odysseus said nothing more, but Telemachus saw his angry face. Would the men see through his father's disguise?

The feast went on into the night. Telemachus wanted the men to go – he longed to speak to his father.

At last, one man stood up and yawned.

'We have had a good feast,' he said. 'I have never laughed so much. But now it is time for bed.'

They all left, laughing and joking. They forgot to take their swords and spears. Soon Odysseus and Telemachus were alone.

'You fooled them, Father!' laughed Telemachus.

'Yes,' said Odysseus, 'but now we must get ready for tomorrow. I must find a way to stop those men. There will be fighting, and we must win! Let's collect all their swords and spears and hide them.'

When they had hidden the swords and spears, Telemachus went upstairs to talk to his mother.

Later that night, Penelope came down to the great hall. Her servants were clearing away the remains of the feast, and a beggar sat alone at the table. Penelope spoke to him.

'My son Telemachus says that you have news of my husband,' said Penelope. 'Tell me what you know.'

'I know that he is safe and well, my lady,' replied the beggar. 'I have seen him with my own eyes.'

'How do I know you are telling the truth?'

'I can remember what he wore, my lady. He wore a long yellow cloak, with a beautiful gold pin …'

'I remember that cloak!' cried Penelope. 'And the gold pin – I gave it to him!'

'He will come back,' the 'beggar' said.

'No – the truth is that I believe I will never see my husband again,' Penelope replied sadly. 'He has been away for too long. But thank you for your kindness.'

CHAPTER 13
A SHOOTING CONTEST

The next day, when the men came back for another feast, they saw the beggar sitting at the table.

'Why is that beggar here again, Telemachus?' asked one man. 'Does he think he is a guest?'

'He *is* a guest,' said Telemachus. 'He is *my* guest. I am Odysseus's son, and this is Odysseus's palace. What do you say to that?'

'I say … I say, let's start our feast! Let's not waste time on a beggar!' said one man.

The feast began. The men were soon laughing and singing and telling jokes.

Suddenly, the door opened. Penelope came in. She was carrying a bow and some arrows in her arms. When she spoke, her voice was cold.

'I have made up my mind,' she said. 'My husband will not come back now, and I am tired of you all. I am tired of your feasting, and your singing, and your offers of marriage. I have decided that I *will* marry one of you. But it will be the man who can shoot arrows with my husband's bow!'

Penelope took a golden cup, and stood it on the table at the end of the great hall.

'You must each take an arrow,' she said. 'Now, let the shooting contest begin!'

The first man fitted his arrow into the bow, and aimed at the golden cup. The arrow flew across the hall – and right out of the window.

Each man took his turn – but no one could hit the cup. And then the beggar spoke.

'Let *me* have a turn,' he said. 'I may be old and ragged – but I can shoot an arrow as well as any man!'

The men laughed, but the beggar fitted an arrow into the bow and pulled back his arm. The arrow flew through the air ... and knocked the cup from the table.

The beggar threw back the hood of his ragged cloak and took another arrow.

'The only man who can shoot with Odysseus's bow – is Odysseus!' he cried, aiming at one of the men. 'And Odysseus is going to shoot again!'

When the men realised that the beggar was really Odysseus, they ran to get their swords and their spears – but they could not find them. The men were so frightened of Odysseus and Telemachus that they ran out of the door and ran away as fast as they could.

When the fight was over, Odysseus ran to Penelope and took her in his arms.

'Yes, it is I, your husband Odysseus!' he cried happily. 'I am home!'

That night, Odysseus told Penelope about his adventures.

'Twelve ships sailed away from Troy …'

THE SEA

The sea is a hungry dog,
Giant and grey.
He rolls on the beach all day.
With his clashing teeth and shaggy jaws
Hour upon hour he gnaws
The rumbling, tumbling stones,
And 'Bones, bones, bones!'
The giant sea-dog moans,
Licking his greasy paws.

And when the night wind roars
and the moon rocks in the stormy cloud,
He bounds to his feet and snuffs and sniffs,
Shaking his wet sides over the cliffs,
And howls and hollos long and loud.

But on quiet days in May or June,
When even the grasses on the dune
Play no more their reedy tune,
With his head between his paws
He lies on the sandy shores,
So quiet, so quiet, he scarcely snores.

James Reeves

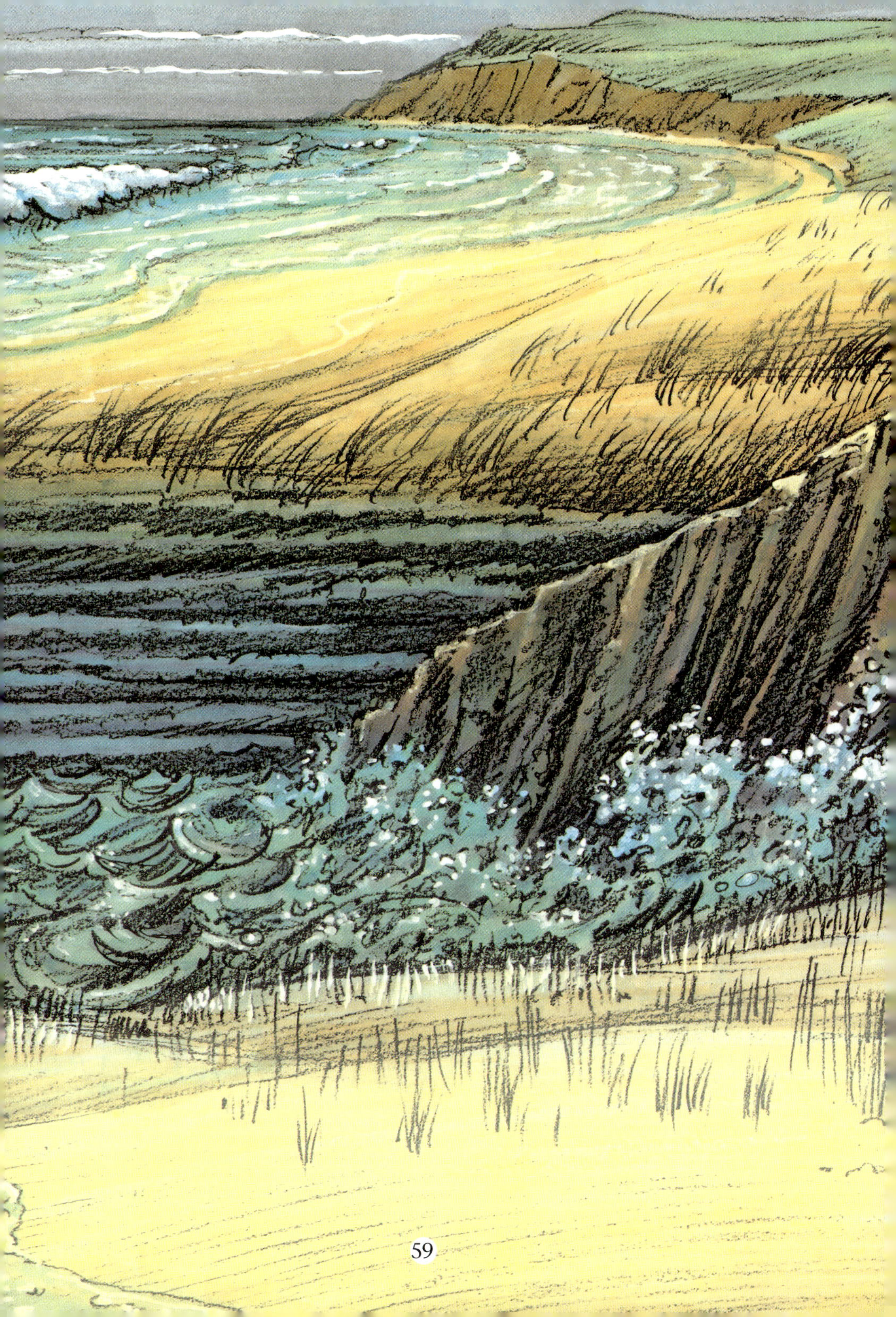

ANCIENT GREECE

The story of Odysseus was first told by the people of Ancient Greece. They lived several thousand years ago, but we know a lot about them from the stories, buildings and art they left behind.

The Ancient Greeks worshipped many gods, and built temples in their honour. The most famous is called the Parthenon. It is in Athens, the capital of Greece.

The most powerful ruler of Ancient Greece was Alexander the Great. He was perhaps the most successful leader in the history of the world.

Greek warriors were very good sailors. The type of ship that Odysseus and his men sail in was called a 'pentekonter'.

The story of Odysseus is one of many Ancient Greek myths. The myths often tell of a hero who has to fight terrible monsters, such as the Minotaur, a creature that is part man and part bull.

The world's most famous athletic contest, the Olympic Games, began in the Ancient Greek city of Olympia.

GREECE TODAY

These photographs show you what the Greek islands are like today.

Lunch in a taverna
(a restaurant)

Fishermen mending
their nets

Holidaymakers enjoying the sun

The remains of a temple on the island of Aegina

A donkey carrying logs for firewoood

The olive harvest

Windsurfing

Macmillan Education
Between Towns Road, Oxford OX4 3PP
A division of Macmillan Publishers Limited
Companies and representatives throughout the world

ISBN 978-1-4050-6016-5

Text © Gill Munton 2007
Design and illustration © Macmillan Publishers Limited 2007

First published 2007

All rights reserved; no part of this publication may be reproduced, stored in a retrieval system, transmitted in any form, or by any means, electronic, mechanical, photocopying, recording, or otherwise, without the prior written permission of the publishers.

Design and layout by Anthony Godber
Illustrated by Peter Simpson
Cover design by Linda Reed & Associates
Cover illustration by Peter Simpson

The Series Editor and the Author would like to give special thanks to Gill McLean for her contribution in setting up the *Macmillan Explorers* series, for her continuous encouragement, and for her positive and practical help and advice throughout its production.

We are grateful for permission to reprint the following copyright material: *The Sea* copyright © James Reeves, from *The Complete Book of Poems for Children* (Heinemann) by permission of the Laura Cecil Literary Agency on behalf of the James Reeves Estate.

The authors and publishers would like to thank the following for permission to reproduce their photographic material:
Alamy/Naglestock.com pp60 (t); Chris A Crumley (bl); Corbis/Tracy Kahan p63 (tr); George Blonsky (b); Ian Dagnall (tl); Jacqui Hurst (br); Leonid Sevebrennikov 62 (b); Mary Evans Picture Library 61 (tl) (tr); Robert Harding Picture Library (tr); Travelshots.com 63 (tl); Visual Arts Library (b)

Printed and bound in Malaysia

2015 2014 2013
10 9